Ten Hits, One Run, Nine Errors

Gospel Sermons For Sundays After Pentecost (Last Third) Cycle C

John E. Berger

CSS Publishing Company, Inc., Lima, Ohio

TEN HITS, ONE RUN, NINE ERRORS

Copyright © 2000 by
CSS Publishing Company, Inc.
Lima, Ohio

All rights reserved. No part of this publication may be reproduced in any manner whatsoever without the prior permission of the publisher, except in the case of brief quotations embodied in critical articles and reviews. Inquiries should be addressed to: Permissions, CSS Publishing Company, Inc., P.O. Box 4503, Lima, Ohio 45802-4503.

Scripture quotations are from the *New Revised Standard Version of the Bible,* copyright 1989 by the Division of Christian Education of the National Council of the Churches of Christ in the USA. Used by permission.

Library of Congress Cataloging-in-Publication Data

Berger, John E., 1929–
   Ten hits, one run, nine errors : Gospel sermons for Sundays after Pentecost (last third), Cycle C / John E. Berger.
     p. cm.
   ISBN 0-7880-1740-3 (alk. paper)
   1. Pentecost season—Sermons. 2. Sermons, American. 3. Bible. N.T. Gospels—Sermons. I. Title.
BV4300.5 B47 2000
252'.64—dc21   00-035802
                                                                                                                       CIP

This book is available in the following formats, listed by ISBN:
   0-7880-1740-3   Book
   0-7880-1741-1   Disk
   0-7880-1742-X   Sermon Prep

For more information about CSS Publishing Company resources, visit our website at www.csspub.com.

PRINTED IN U.S.A.

Dedicated to

The Twelve Churches I Love The Most:

Emmanuel Lutheran Church, North Georgetown, Ohio
— the church of my parents and grandparents

Grace Lutheran Church, Springfield, Ohio
— where I was baptized

St. Luke Lutheran Church, Lima, Ohio — where I was confirmed

Rockway Lutheran Church, Springfield, Ohio
— where Mary Frances Kantonen and I were married

Messiah Lutheran Church, Newton Falls, Ohio
— my first pastorate

Mount Moriah Lutheran Church, Berlin Center, Ohio
— where I was Stated Supply Pastor, 1958-1961

St. Lucas Lutheran Church, Toledo, Ohio
— where I was pastor for 34 years

and to my Interim Pastor congregations
which have made my retirement so happy:

Christ Lutheran Church (Dowling), Bowling Green, Ohio

Salem Lutheran Church, Pemberville, Ohio

St. John Lutheran Church, Montpelier, Ohio

St. John Lutheran Church, Findlay, Ohio

St. Paul Lutheran Church, McClure, Ohio

Table Of Contents

Proper 23   7
Pentecost 21
Ordinary Time 28
    Ten Hits, One Run, Nine Errors
    Luke 17:11-19

Proper 24   13
Pentecost 22
Ordinary Time 29
    Don't Hang Up On God
    Luke 18:1-8

Proper 25   19
Pentecost 23
Ordinary Time 30
    Good Guys And Bad Guys
    Luke 18:9-14

Proper 26   25
Pentecost 24
Ordinary Time 31
    Sorry Enough To Quit
    Luke 19:1-10

Proper 27   31
Pentecost 25
Ordinary Time 32
    God, The Ultimate Professional
    Luke 20:27-38

Proper 28   37
Pentecost 26
Ordinary Time 33
    Do Right; Trust God
    Luke 21:5-19

All Saints' Sunday 41
    Golden Rule Saints
    Luke 6:20-31

Christ The King Sunday 47
    The Throne Of The Cross
    Luke 23:33-43

Thanksgiving Day 51
    For What God Has Given
    John 6:25-35

Lectionary Preaching After Pentecost 57

Proper 23 • *Pentecost 21* • *Ordinary Time 28*

Ten Hits, One Run, Nine Errors

Luke 17:11-19

A map of the Holy Land In Jesus' day looked like this: Galilee at the top, Judea at the bottom, and sandwiched in between: Samaria.

For unpleasant reasons of history, religion, and racism, the Jews of Galilee and of Judea looked down on the Samaritans; and Samaritans were unfriendly to Jews. Like so many historical hatreds, they were not sensible. Sensible or not, the favorite route of travel between Judea in the South and Galilee in the North was an end run to the East. Better to walk miles out of the way than to walk directly through Samaria.

Included in Jesus' ministry was overcoming this hatred. Thus the hero of a parable was the Good Samaritan; and the "woman at the well" was a Samaritan. In today's Gospel only one out of ten healed lepers returned to say thanks, "and he was a Samaritan."

There is another lesson against racism, easily overlooked, in today's Gospel: Jewish lepers had no problem getting along with a Samaritan leper. In their common misery and humiliation, lepers found brotherhood and sisterhood no matter what their race or religion.

Leprosy was a disgusting and incurable disease. Even without the benefit of scientific medicine those almost 2,000-years-ago people observed that there was something communicable about leprosy. As a precaution against infecting others, lepers were condemned to being outcasts outside town. They would have starved if it were not for gifts of food left by loved ones — always at a safe distance, however.

Jesus' fame as a healer had spread to this miserable cluster of lepers. "Jesus, Master, have mercy on us!" they shouted. Today's Gospel notes that they did so, "keeping their distance." Jesus' response was only seven words: "Go and show yourselves to the priests."

Priests were the public health officers of their day. If a leper believed that he or she had gotten miraculously well, or perhaps the sickness had been misdiagnosed, the priests were the persons to approve or to disapprove a certificate of good health.

All ten lepers deserve some credit for faith in Jesus, because they all started walking! No questions were asked, and no explanations were demanded. They just started walking, and they saw a wonderful change in their bodies. Gray and decaying flesh changed to flesh-color and healthy-looking. They were healed.

Having just been healed, what would go through a person's mind? Going home and surprising the family, perhaps. Maybe returning to work, and hoping that employers and customers would accept the priests' declaration of wellness. Or getting a bath and some decent clothes. Probably low on the list of priorities would be, "I should take time to say, 'Thank You, Jesus.' " But one person did, "and he was a Samaritan."

How fortunate we are, if we have developed a "thanks attitude" so that we feel and say "thanks" immediately — both to people and to God.

A basketball coach instructed his players that whenever they made a basket with assistance from a teammate, they should signal a thank you message with a gesture or some kind of salute. "But, coach, what if the other player isn't looking in our direction?" one player asked. "Don't worry; he will be," was the answer. We all like to be thanked.

A pastor, eight years after his graduation, remembered a college teacher who had been especially helpful. Remembering that he had never expressed gratitude to this man, the pastor wrote a letter to express his thanks and his apologies for waiting so long. The pastor never received an answer, probably because two months later the alumni magazine announced the professor's death. The pastor hoped his letter had arrived in time to be understood and enjoyed. Better late than never, but why not develop a "thanks attitude" to do it right immediately?

Saint Luke, the author of today's Gospel, was a doctor by profession before he became the personal physician and traveling companion of Saint Paul, as well as a writer whose most famous published books are "The Gospel According to Saint Luke" and its companion volume "The Acts of the Apostles." Let us imagine Doctor Luke, M.D., writing this letter to Ann Landers, newspaper advice columnist.

> *Dear Ann Landers:*
> *As a doctor I thought I was accustomed to having lots of complaining patients, and very few words of gratitude. But recently I heard an experience that shocked even me.*
> *Ten people sick with leprosy were healed by Jesus; I call him the Great Healer. Not only did they not pay anything for Jesus' house call; only one took time to say "thanks."*
> *Signed, Hopping Mad in Antioch*
>
> *Dear Hopping Mad:*
> *I hear you, and thanks for the reminder that we all need a "thanks attitude."*
> *At the same time, people who deal with the public need to remember that most people do not mean to be ungrateful; people get busy and forgetful. You know it; I know it; certainly Jesus knew it.*

"Your faith has made you well," Jesus told the grateful Samaritan. What did Jesus mean, when the Ungrateful Nine were just as healed? There was no punishment for their ingratitude or forgetfulness. He must have meant that healing meant more to this one man, and it would be part of his life's faith experience.

In *Gone with the Wind* sweet Melaine Wilkes donated her wedding ring to a fund raiser for the Confederate Army. "It may help my husband," she said. Rhett Butler, ordinarily unsentimental, was deeply moved; "I know how much that means to you." Not to be outdone, Scarlett O'Hara, an ungrieving widow, flippantly tossed her wedding ring into the collection box. Returning to his normal cynicism, Rhett Butler observed, "And I know how much that means to you, Scarlett." (Not much, really.)

So it was with the ten former-lepers. All ten were healed, but to the Samaritan it meant something more.

This healing miracle is a wonderful illustration of Martin Luther's explanation of the Lord's Prayer's Fourth Petition, "Give us this day our daily bread." Luther wrote: "God gives daily bread, even without our prayer, to all people, though sinful, but we ask in this prayer that he will help us to realize this and to receive our daily bread with thanks."

Most important, perhaps, in this miracle is another example of Jesus' compassion and his healing power. It brings to mind that old Sunday school song, "I think, when I read that sweet story of old, when Jesus was here among men ... I should like to have been with them then."

Today we believe that God shows his miraculous healing through medicine. An encyclopedia article about leprosy describes medicines with names like Dapsone, Avlosulfon, Lamprene, and Rifamycin. More recent encyclopedias would probably tell about even newer and more effective prescriptions.

Those who are old enough will remember the summertime fears of polio, also known as infantile paralysis. Others will remember when pneumonia meant death. "Broken hip" was once sadly a sure sign of invalidism, physical decline, and death for the elderly. Most of our communities have old buildings, abandoned or converted, which old-timers still call "TB hospitals." These were not ancient diseases like the Black Plague of the so-called Dark Ages. Ask your parents and grandparents.

"Ten Hits, One Run, Nine Errors" is the title of this sermon. "Ten Hits": Jesus healed ten people of leprosy. Ten acts of mercy, and ten opportunities for gratitude.

"One Run": only one person had enough "Thanks Attitude" to say, "Thank You," to Jesus. To our Lord he must have seemed like a baseball game's "hit."

"Nine Errors": nine people without a proper "Thanks Attitude." Like a baseball game's lost opportunities, they were "nine errors."

Tonight when you are saying your bedtime prayers, stop thinking, for a little while at least, about all the worries we still have. Think, for a little while at least, about all the worries God has taken care of for us. Then praise God with a loud voice, prostrate yourself at Jesus' feet, and thank him.

Proper 24 • *Pentecost 22* • *Ordinary Time 29*

Don't Hang Up On God

Luke 18:1-8

Did Jesus ever do comedy? Indeed he did, and the Parable of the Unjust Judge is partly comic monologue. The routine began with a probate judge so ridiculously dishonest that he announced, "... I have no fear of God and no respect for anyone...." (There must have been a gasp of disbelief from Jesus' audience.)

The Unjust Judge was nagged by a widow, however, who had every right to nag, because she had been cheated by somebody in the community. A good judge would have helped the widow, but remember, this judge "neither feared God nor had respect for people."

The widow made a project of picking at the Unjust Judge for justice. Whenever he stepped out of his house she was there, demanding justice in a voice loud enough to be heard by neighbors and passers-by. She followed him along the street while he was on his way to court. Even at night this widow stood outside the judge's house to denounce him to the community, and to disturb his sleep. (By this time in Jesus' story-telling there must have been a few chuckles from the audience.)

Even the Unjust Judge's wife and children suffered from the harassment. At last the Unjust Judge relented, not from any desire to do the right thing, but, as he himself said, " ... because this widow keeps bothering me. I will grant her justice, so that she may not wear me out by continually coming." (By this time in Jesus' story there must have been laughter.)

The Parable of the Unjust Judge was a negative illustration, just as a tennis coach might demonstrate incorrectly awkward motions to his or her team: "This is *not* the way to play tennis."

Or a marriage counselor might give husbands and wives examples of what *not* to say in a loving relationship.

As a negative illustration the Parable of the Unjust Judge teaches that God is *not* like the Unjust Judge. Instead God gives justice to widows, to orphans, and to you and to me.

Not mere justice, actually. What God gives us is much, much more than justice. God gives us unearned blessings far above "justice."

During the Civil War a Confederate soldier was put on trial in a place where General Robert E. Lee himself was one of the military judges. "Don't be nervous, son; you will get justice here," General Lee tried to set the soldier at ease. "That is exactly what I am afraid of, General," was the reply.

We too would have reason to be nervous, if we could expect only "justice" from God. As a matter of Christian fact, however, we get new chances to pick up broken pieces from our sinful failures — to try again. And as a matter of another fact, we receive new opportunities and new gifts from God which make the Unjust Judge's performance seem extra harsh and unfair.

The Parable of the Unjust Judge is also a lesson for our being persistent in our faith in God.

A religious road sign near Hoosic, New York, says, "When God puts you on hold, do not hang up." The widow in the parable was persistent; she did not "hang up."

Jacob in the Old Testament was persistent in his midnight wrestling match. His mysterious opponent said:

> *"Let me go, for the day is breaking." But Jacob said, "I will not let you go, unless you bless me." So he said to him, "What is your name?" And he said, "Jacob." Then the man said, "You shall no longer be called Jacob, but Israel, for you have striven with God and with humans, and have prevailed."*
> — Genesis 32:26-28

In the story of God's destruction of the wicked city of Sodom, Abraham successfully haggled God into a promise to spare the city if as few as ten righteous persons could be found.

> *Will you indeed sweep away the righteous with the wicked? Suppose there are fifty righteous within the city; will you then sweep away the place and not forgive it for the fifty righteous who are in it? Far be it from you to do such a thing, to slay the righteous with the wicked, so that the righteous fare as the wicked! Far be that from you! Shall not the Judge of all the earth do what is just?* — Genesis 18:23-33

Abraham persuaded God to lower the magic number to forty, to thirty, to twenty, and finally to ten. As it turned out, not even ten righteous people lived in Sodom, so the destruction took place. But consider the concept: Abraham argued with God! Abraham dared to lecture God about what was right: "Far be that from you! Shall not the Judge of all the earth do what is just?"

In the Old Testament story of Moses receiving the Ten Commandments on two slabs of stone, while he was up on Mount Sinai, the Israelites grew tired of waiting. In the absence of Moses they worshiped a golden calf, and God was so angry about their idolatry that he told Moses, "Now let me alone, so that my wrath may burn hot against them and I may consume them ..." (Exodus 32:10). Like Abraham, Moses argued with God: "Turn from your fierce wrath; change your mind and do not bring disaster on your people" (Exodus 32:12b).

Exodus 32:14 says, "And the Lord changed his mind about the disaster that he planned to bring on his people." Once again, "When God puts you on hold, do not hang up."

Jesus himself admired the persistence of the Canaanite woman. When she asked for healing of her sick daughter, Jesus at first ignored her. Then, "I was sent only to the lost sheep of the house of Israel" (not to Gentile-Canaanites like you). Then he said, "It is not fair to take the children's food and throw it to the dogs."

"Yes," the woman said, "yet even the dogs eat the crumbs that fall from their masters' table." "Then Jesus answered her, 'Woman, great is your faith! Let it be done for you as you wish.' And her daughter was healed instantly" (Matthew 15:21-28).

We do not know why Jesus was so harshly out-of-character with the Canaanite woman. There are different explanations, but the point here is that Jesus admired her persistence. When Jesus "put her on hold" she did not "hang up."

Martin Luther suffered from depression and doubts all his life. He comforted himself by saying, "I am baptized." And again, "I dispute much with God with great impatience, and I hold him to his promises."

Even after all these examples of arguing with God, however, most of us are allowed to be more comfortable in accepting God's answers to our prayers and learning to live with them. We are not required to wrestle with God, nor to lecture God, nor to try to force God to change his mind.

We can follow the example of Jesus in the Garden of Gethsemane: "... not what I want but what you want" (Matthew 26:39b). Because God is not like the Unjust Judge, we can quietly follow the widow's example of persistence in the parable by praying the Third Petition of the Lord's Prayer: "Thy will be done on earth as it is in heaven."

If you have memorized Luther's explanation of this Third Petition of the Lord's Prayer, you will remember these words: "The good and gracious will of God is done even without our prayer, but we pray in this petition that it may be done among us also."

You might ask: What should be our attitude toward prayer when God seems to put us on hold? We should, of course, pray for what we want and need — and then take time to listen for God's answer.

A teacher from the Alban Institute told a group of pastors that we church people are reasonably good at praying good prayers with beautiful words and good thoughts. We mistakenly consider the prayer ended, however, after we have stopped talking and said "Amen."

We have handed God a one-way radio, so to speak, with God's end being the receiver only. So the teacher instructed the class to observe ten minutes of absolute silence — eyes closed and minds empty of busy thought. No background music. No words spoken. Just silence.

By the end of the ten minutes there was a feeling of some serenity and more peace. There were no visions of heaven, but feelings that God's will could be better understood — if we just took more time to listen.

God is not like the Unjust Judge. God is good to us. Sometimes it takes patience and openness to God's will for us to understand how our prayers are answered.

Proper 25 • Pentecost 23 • Ordinary Time 30

Good Guys And Bad Guys

Luke 18:9-14

Today's sermon begins with this little one-person drama.

> *As I stand here in this pulpit today, I am glad that I am not like that bad Pharisee. I never pray out loud just so people can see me, and hear me, and be impressed by my religious words. I give money to church, but I never boast about it. I go to church and Sunday school almost every Sunday, but I never brag about that, either — like the Pharisee did. Instead I am very humble, as the tax collector was. Just like the tax collector, I say, "God, be merciful to me a sinner!" That's the reason God sends me home justified, because "all who humble themselves will be exalted."*

This little drama makes the point that it is foolish and wrong for us to come before God with haughty attitudes about anything — even our humility. In the sight of God we are all truly empty-handed — both Pharisee and tax collector.

Giving credit where it is due, the Pharisee was at least trying to be godly — at a time when so few people were even trying. How sad that his efforts at godliness made him so arrogant and unlovable. Not only was he an offense to God; he set such an ugly example that ordinary people would not want to imitate him. That was a bad kind of "evangelism."

The Pharisee was like a cartoon of Garfield the cat. Standing front-and-center on the stage of a Broadway musical, dressed in tap dance shoes and white trousers and straw hat, swinging a cane, loving the applause and spotlight — Garfield says, "It is hard to be humble, when you're as great as I am." If it were not that the Pharisee took himself so seriously, he would have looked as ridiculous as Garfield the cat.

There was a pastor who was successful and confident. Under his leadership his congregation grew. Unfortunately, he was also proud and conceited; and he even persuaded the members of his church that they were the best in town. (Great for them, but hurtful to everybody else.) "It is hard to be humble, when you are as great as we are" was their attitude.

So much for the Pharisee. Now, the tax collector.

Giving blame where it is due, the tax collector was probably correct in his confession, "God, be merciful to me a sinner!"

The typical tax collector was greedy, dishonest, cruel, traitorous, and hard-boiled — and that was on a *good* day. No wonder that Zacchaeus, the short tax collector who climbed a sycamore tree to see Jesus, felt the need to change his ways. "Look, half of my possessions, Lord, I will give to the poor; and if I have defrauded anyone of anything, I will pay back four times as much" (Luke 19:8).

Matthew, a tax collector before he became a disciple, must have been hoping for a better life when he walked away from his hated and hateful profession to follow Jesus. "As Jesus was walking along, he saw a man called Matthew sitting at the tax booth, and he said to him, 'Follow me.' And he got up and followed him" (Matthew 9:9).

Winston Churchill, a colorful and flamboyant prime minister of England, had a political rival named Clement Attlee who was almost the opposite of Churchill. Although hard-working and honest, Attlee lacked the "pizzazz" we sometimes call charisma. "Attlee is a sheep in wolf's clothing," Churchill said of his rival, thus reversing the usual accusation, *"wolf* in *sheep's* clothing."

On another occasion a defender of Attlee said, "At least Attlee is humble." Churchill's response was, "Attlee has a great deal to be humble about."

In today's Parable of the Pharisee and the tax collector, we can admire the humble confession of the tax collector, while recognizing that the tax collector had a great deal to be humble about.

Benjamin Franklin once made a project of improving himself, and he wrote down thirteen good characteristics to work on. "Temperance, Silence, and Order; Resolution, Frugality, and Industry; Sincerity, Justice, and Moderation; Tranquility, Cleanliness, and Chastity; Last of all — Humility." "Imitate Jesus and Socrates," Benjamin Franklin wrote.

Franklin worked on one virtue every week, by keeping a small notebook in which he would mark a black dot every time he backslid. If he found himself overeating, he put one black dot beside the "Temperance" in his little book.

By his second week, Franklin worked on "Silence." "Speak not but what may benefit others or yourself," he wrote. "Avoid trifling conversation." Then he followed the same score-keeping procedure with his little notebook and the black dots.

He was making real progress, he thought. Every week the accumulation of black dots became smaller and smaller. Franklin went on to Order, Resolution, Frugality, and so on; but when he came to the thirteenth week, Humility, Franklin's self-help plan broke down, because he could not avoid being proud of his successful pursuit of Industry, Sincerity, Justice, and all those other good things.

Even Jesus in his Sermon on the Mount urged his followers to let their lights shine: "In the same way, let your light shine before others, so that they may see your good works and give glory to your Father in Heaven" (Matthew 5:16). In our Sunday schools we teach our children to sing, "This little light of mine, I'm gonna let it shine ... Hide it under a basket? No! I'm gonna let it shine ... Don't let Satan blow it out, I'm gonna let it shine."

Our evangelism committees like us to wear Christian jewelry for evangelistic conversation starters: perhaps a fish from Christian symbolism, or "W.W.J.D." (What would Jesus do?).

Contradictory though it may sound, a bit of old-time advice is helpful here: "Hide when tempted to show; show when tempted to hide." In other words, if we start to enjoy too much telling others about our spiritual accomplishments, then back down a bit.

On the other hand, if nobody would guess that we are Christians, we had better express ourselves more. "Hide when tempted to show; show when tempted to hide."

On the fiftieth anniversary of a high school reunion, all the alumni were invited to write small paragraphs about themselves. Some were proud of the rank and income they had achieved in the business world. Others told about their many travels around the world. Still others about the accomplishments of their children and grandchildren. One wrote about herself and her husband, "We spend time, each day, thanking God for all the gifts he has given and continues to give us." God is probably pleased with that much quiet testimony of his goodness.

This sermon is titled "Good Guys And Bad Guys." It comes from a favorite play-time which young boys used to enjoy — and probably still do. "Let's play 'Good guys and bad guys,' " somebody would say. The good guys could be cops; the bad guys, robbers: "Cops and Robbers."

It would be too easy in today's Gospel Lesson to call the Pharisee a "Bad Guy," and the tax collector a "Good Guy." Sad to say, it is human nature for us to assume that we are Good Guys, and other people are Bad Guys. Today's lesson teaches that we all need to pray, "God, be merciful to me, a sinner!"

Knowing how to say, "I'm sorry," or "My fault," to each other would be a good follow-up of this parable. Several newspaper writers invited public suggestions for suitable gestures of "I'm sorry" or "My fault" from one automobile driver to another. We are altogether too familiar with gestures of anger and defiance; but do we know how to communicate something pleasant?

One suggestion — the driver who made the mistake should lower his head slightly and bonk himself on the forehead with the side of the closed fist. The message is clear: "I shouldn't have done that."

A second suggestion — the universal gesture for surrender or forgiveness is to smile and raise both arms, palms outward. If your car is still moving, you should only do this for a brief second.

A third suggestion — when you goof in traffic, give yourself two light thumps on your chest meaning, "I'm at fault."

With proper adjustment of attitudes, the Pharisees of the world and the tax collectors of the world could learn to help each other and perhaps even learn to like each other. That would make God very happy.

Proper 26 • Pentecost 24 • Ordinary Time 31

Sorry Enough To Quit

Luke 19:1-10

Zacchaeus has been a favorite Bible character. His short height seemed cute. His climbing a sycamore tree for better viewing seemed comical. Jesus' calling him by name gave him celebrity. The unpleasant grumbling of onlookers made him an underdog. His enthusiastic intention to give to the poor made him born-again. Finally the greatest tribute came from Jesus himself: "Today salvation has come to this house...."

In short — perhaps we should say, in summary — Zacchaeus has seemed like a cuddly teddy bear. A children's Sunday school song complete with hand motions says,

> *Zacchaeus was a wee little man*
> *A wee little man was he,*
> *He climbed up in a sycamore tree*
> *For the Lord he wanted to see;*
> *And as the Saviour passed that way,*
> *He looked up in the tree,*
> *And he said,*
> *"Zacchaeus, you come down,*
> *For I'm going to your house today.*
> *For I'm going to your house today."*

Zacchaeus' teddy bear image suffers, however, from a definition of the two words "tax" and "collector" in a Bible study.

> *The tax collector was an agent of the foreign imperial government, and he worked against his fellow citizens.*

> *The words "tax collectors" and "sinners" form a usual pair: "tax-collectors-and-sinners." The morality of the tax collectors is presumed to be at the lowest level.*

Furthermore, today's Gospel Lesson describes Zacchaeus as being a *chief* tax collector and as being *rich*. Whatever it was that tax collectors did, Zacchaeus was good at it; and it made him quite successful.

Then there came the power of redemption through Jesus. Zacchaeus was the very kind of person Jesus had been looking for: the *up*-and-out. Much of Jesus' ministry had been focused on the more familiar *down*-and-out: the poor, the sick, and the outcast. Zacchaeus represented something different; he was rich and successful. True, he was unpopular; and most people then and now prefer to be liked, although some say they do not care, because they can "cry all the way to the bank!" For most of us — including probably Zacchaeus — "Sticks and stones can break my bones, but words can break my heart."

Perhaps hidden inside Zacchaeus was a guilty conscience. Perhaps it bothered him that he had cheated and hurt so many people. At any rate he welcomed the opportunity for a new chance in life. He volunteered to reform and to repay his victims. In present-day law we would say that Zacchaeus offered to pay restitution and to perform community service.

It would have been better if Zacchaeus had not used the word "if": "... and *if* I have defrauded anyone of anything...." Recent Christian journalists point out the cheapening effect of the word "if" in so many present-day apologies. "*If* I hurt your feelings, I am sorry." "*If* I did something wrong, I am sorry." The word "if" turns an apology into a non-apology.

Let us give Zacchaeus the benefit of the doubt. He showed signs of big improvement, and Jesus was happy for it.

The grumbling of the onlookers was unfortunate. They might have gotten tax reform and more honest treatment from Zacchaeus and his underlings at tax time, if only they had been more receptive of the new Zacchaeus.

A preacher who likes to tell children's sermons made two cardboard faces from the Zacchaeus story. One was a happy face with the mouth curved upward in a smile. The other was a disapproving face with the mouth curled downward in a permanent scowl. The happy face was labeled "Mrs. Good-and-Nice"; the scowling face was labeled "Mr. Good-but-Nasty." The children's sermon said that it is important to be "good," but it is also important to be "nice" to people. The onlookers who grumbled about Jesus' befriending Zacchaeus may have been "good," but they were "nasty."

Sometimes new Christians can be boring and offensive when they brag about how bad they were before they were saved. They seem to belittle lifelong Christians who never experienced such wicked, wicked ways in the first place. Nevertheless, when a sinner reforms — whether it is Saul before he became Saint Paul, or Zacchaeus, or you, or me — it should be an occasion for joy among all God's people.

There was a Sunday school lesson on the word "repentance." "What does 'repentance' mean?" the teacher asked. "Being sorry for your sins," was one answer. Not bad, but better still was, "Being sorry enough to quit." How wonderful that Zacchaeus was not only sorry for his sins, he was sorry enough to quit.

"No U-turn" is a familiar traffic sign to automobile drivers. "No U-turn" is usually posted at cross-over places on median strips of multi-lane highways. The cross-overs are reserved for emergency vehicles like police cars, fire trucks, and ambulances; but the rest of us are warned to keep going straight ahead until the next exit.

Imagine the surprise of a pastor, new in his community, to see "U-turn *permitted*" on a traffic sign at the end of a railroad underpass. There were so few exit streets in the neighborhood, he learned, that this U-turn was considered necessary.

The preacher thought about that unusual traffic sign "U-turn permitted"; but then he took it a step further for his next sermon. When it comes to sin, he thought, there should be spiritual traffic signs: "U-turn *recommended*" or even "U-turn *expected*" or "U-turn *required*." It is not enough to be sorry for our sins; we need to be sorry enough to quit, to U-turn away from sin.

Some social critics lament that we live in a time of "new immorality" — when sinners are not sorry for sin, and they have no intention of changing. One such sinner boasts that his belief is based upon the hymn "Just as I am." "God must accept me 'just as I am.' " There you have it: no need for restitution for sin, because God is supposed to accept him "just as he is." No need for being "sorry enough to quit," if God accepts him "just as he is." No need to make a U-turn away from sin, if God accepts everybody "just as I am."

Some prosecuting attorneys complain that they have difficulty getting jury convictions these days, because of what they call "television talk show syndrome." Talk show hosts may ask a guest what his reasons were for killing his father. "Because he abused me when I was little" might be the answer — which makes television viewers all over the country sympathetic with the murderer. This kind of program has influenced people — including juries — to decide "not guilty for reason of something" in cases of murder, theft, perjury, or anything else. Unfortunately it makes "I am depraved, on account of I was deprived" an excuse for believing "accept me 'just as I am' — neither confession nor restitution necessary."

Imagine, if you will, Zacchaeus saying, "I am a dishonest tax collector, because I am so short. People made fun of me, so I became a tax collector to get even with people."

For many years the favorite Bible verse was John 3:16, "For God so loved the world that he gave his only Son, so that everyone who believes in him may not perish but may have eternal life." Before that it was Psalm 23:1, "The Lord is my shepherd, I shall not want."

Today's favorite Bible verse seems to be Matthew 7:1, "Do not judge, so that you may not be judged." It was a great Bible verse, to be sure, until it became twisted and abused by Satan to harden our hearts and to dull our sense of right and wrong.

Billy Graham has preached about God's view of tolerance. Billy Graham says that tolerance has become too stretched, that Jesus actually was *narrow* about the way of salvation. Jesus was intolerant toward hypocrisy, intolerant toward selfishness, and intolerant toward sin.

Have you ever wondered what became of Zacchaeus? There is no evidence that he became a disciple of Jesus, as Matthew, another tax collector, did. Perhaps he returned to his old dishonest ways by saying, "I must have gotten emotionally swept away when I was with Jesus. Besides, if I don't do it, somebody else will."

It would be wonderful if he continued his tax collecting office but became an inspiring example of doing it right. Maybe on the other hand he decided there was no way to be an *honest* tax collector, so had a mid-life crisis instead and went into something cleaner and more satisfying.

We do not know how Zacchaeus turned out, or what he did next. We do know that the final verse in today's lesson is a powerful conclusion: "For the Son of Man came to seek out and to save the lost" — like Zacchaeus, and you, and me.

Proper 27 • *Pentecost 25* • *Ordinary Time 32*

God, The Ultimate Professional

Luke 20:27-38

Here is a true story about a strange funeral service.

The deceased man had no church home, but that is not the unusual part of the story. The man's widow asked for a certain clergyman to be the funeral preacher. The desired clergyman had performed a family wedding a few years earlier. That is not unusual either. It is what is called "an extended church family relationship." In other words, the man had been neither a church member nor a church goer, but there had been a connecting experience — in this case a family wedding.

So far in the story there would be nothing terribly unusual. The unusual part was that the widow wanted no mention of resurrection in the pastor's sermon, Bible lessons, or prayers. There should be nothing about life after death, heaven, or reunion with loved ones. No Bible readings like John 11:25, "I am the resurrection and the life. Those who believe in me, even though they die, will live...."

She wanted nothing like John 14:2-3, "In my Father's house there are many dwelling places ... And if I go and prepare a place for you, I will come again and take you to myself...."

The widow did not want any prayers for her husband like, "(O Lord) receive him into the arms of your mercy ... and into the glorious company of the saints in light. Amen."

The reason she gave to the startled and dismayed pastor was this: "I am his third wife. He outlived the first two wives. Which one of us would be his wife in the next world?"

The widow did not know the Bible well enough to recognize today's Gospel Lesson, but the similarity to Luke 20:33 is striking: "In the resurrection, therefore, whose wife will the woman be? For the seven had married her." (There are differences in details, of course. In the Gospel lesson it was the *woman* who had outlived *seven* husbands.)

There is still one more strange twist to this funeral story. The widow, who was really grieving, had invited a personal friend of the family to sing two of their favorite "songs": "Just A Closer Walk With Thee" and "Amazing Grace." The officiating clergyman wondered what the widow would think when the soloist came to the verses

> *When my feeble life is o'er'*
> *Time for me will be no more;*
> *On that bright eternal shore*
> *I will walk, dear Lord, close to Thee*
>   — (from "Just A Closer Walk With Thee")

and

> *When we've been there 10,000 years*
> *Bright shining as the sun,*
> *We've no less days to sing God's praise*
> *Than when we'd first begun*
>   — (from "Amazing Grace").

He need not have been concerned, the minister said; the widow loved the songs — every note and every word. All of which made him wonder, "Do people really listen to the words of the gospel hymns we Christians hold so dear? Do they care?"

Now back to the Gospel for today. When the Sadducees told their made-up story and asked Jesus their trick question — "... whose wife will the woman be?" — it was their intention to make Jesus look foolish. They did not like Jesus anyway, and they themselves did not believe in life after death.

Interestingly, this no-life-after-death belief of the Sadducees appears again in Acts 23:6-10, when Saint Paul was able to turn the Sadducees and Pharisees against each other. In most respects the Pharisees were anti-Jesus and anti-Paul — except that the Pharisees *did* believe in life after death. Paul was able to win himself a few friends by declaring, "Brothers, I am a Pharisee, a son of Pharisees. I am on trial concerning the hope of the resurrection of the dead." Then the Pharisees became temporary supporters of Paul: "We find nothing wrong with this man. What if a spirit or an angel has spoken to him?"

Those of us who believe in life after death would like to know more, much more, about the next world. Animal lovers have wondered, "Will my pet be in heaven with me?" People who like to eat ask, "What kind of food will be served in heaven?" Men and women with physical disabilities hope they will have glorified bodies. How will we use all that time in eternity? What kind of clothing will people wear? What age will we appear to be?

Happily married people wonder, "Will I live with my wife?" "Will I live with my husband?"

Basically the answer to all these questions is, "Trust God. God has good answers to questions and problems we have not even thought of."

When people consult a professional (dentist, physician, attorney, insurance agent, plumber, auto mechanic, and so on), there is usually a feeling of confidence, or no confidence. We either feel that this professional has our needs well in hand, or not.

There was a machine shop foreman who claimed he could tell if a new employee was any good just from the way he or she turned on the power switch of the machine!

A band director claimed she could tell if a new musician was any good just from the tuning-up and warming-up of the band instrument.

God is the Ultimate Professional! Naturally, we would like to know more, much more, and right now, about heavenly details. We need to be satisfied, however, with the trust shown by David in his Twenty-third Psalm: "even though I walk through the darkest valley, I fear no evil; for you are with me...."

A man confessed with both amusement and embarrassment to one of his childhood worries: What would he wear for adult-size clothing "on the morning he awoke to find himself fully grown, suddenly and overnight"? Would he hide his nakedness by staying under bed covers, while his parents hurried to the store to buy adult-size underwear, trousers, shirts, and socks to replace his childish and outgrown sizes? The man said it required considerable assurance from his parents that he need not worry about this problem.

To God our questions and worries about the next world must seem equally silly. God is indeed the Ultimate Professional about the next world. God has good answers to questions and problems we have not even thought of yet.

A dying bishop said, "I will not be alive in the spring. But I will soon experience new life in a different way. Although I do not know what to expect in the afterlife, I do know that God is now calling me home."

He recalled that when, as an adult, he visited for the first time his parents' ancestral village in Europe, he felt that he had been there before. After years of looking through his parents' photo albums, he felt that he knew the mountains, the land, the houses, and the people. Then as he thought about his own upcoming death, he decided that crossing from this life into eternal life would be similar. He would be home in heaven, a place he had never seen; but he had read about heaven in the Bible, and he had confidence in Jesus' promises.

To Saint Paul believing in life after death was not — and is not — a matter of choice for Christians. Neither is belief in heaven a matter of mere wishful thinking. Belief in heaven is a requirement of the Christian faith.

"Now if Christ is proclaimed as raised from the dead, how can some of you say there is no resurrection of the dead?" Saint Paul asked. (See 1 Corinthians 15:12-26.) "If there is no resurrection of the dead, then Christ has not been raised; and if Christ has not been raised, then our proclamation has been in vain and your faith has been in vain."

Then Saint Paul became most emphatic: "If for this life only we have hope in Christ, we are of all people most to be pitied. But in fact Christ has been raised from the dead, the first fruit of those who have died."

Today, November 11, is the eighty-third anniversary of the ending of World War I. "The eleventh hour, of the eleventh day, of the eleventh month" is the way it was described. On November 11, 1918, at 11:00 in the morning there was an armistice to end four years of war in France. Veterans said that German and Austrian soldiers on one side, and French, British, and American soldiers on the other side, cautiously climbed up and out of their opposing trenches; and then they all met their former enemies in the middle of "no man's land" to celebrate together that the war was over.

For years afterward November 11 was remembered in the United States as Armistice Day; and as Day of Remembrance in other English-speaking countries.

It had been hoped that November 11, 1918, would mark "the War to end wars," but sadly there followed World War II, the Korean War, the Vietnam War, Desert Storm, and does the list continue?

So the commemoration on November 11 changed to pay tribute to our veterans of all wars, not just World War I. It is appropriate that today Veterans Day is an occasion for us to remember our Christian belief in life after death.

At an evangelistic revival some years ago, the preacher assured his listeners of Jesus' promise, "The one who believes and is baptized will be saved ..." (Mark 16:16). Then he told people to turn to the persons nearby, to shake hands, and to say, "I'll see you in heaven" ... "I'll see you in heaven" ... "I'll see you in heaven."

I conclude with a key verse from today's Gospel lesson, Luke 20:38, "Now he is God not of the dead, but of the living; for to him all of them are alive."

Proper 28 • *Pentecost 26* • *Ordinary Time 33*

Do Right; Trust God

Luke 21:5-19

In the moving picture *Planet of the Apes* the viewing audience is led to believe that a United States rocket ship has crash-landed on another planet, which the flight crew is horrified to discover is inhabited and ruled by super-apes. These super-apes speak perfect English, wear stylish clothes, live in cities, and in many respects are just as accomplished as human earthlings. There are even super-ape churches, where the super-ape-pastors preach on texts like "Ape shall not kill ape," and "I never met an ape I did not like."

The astronauts discover something stranger and even more frightening, however. There are some humanlike creatures on the same planet, but they have somehow become brutish and subhuman. Indeed the super-apes raise them as cattle to be eaten, or as wild game to be hunted. The stranded astronauts, not yet discovered by the super-apes, realize that if they are seen, they will be hunted and rounded up and dehumanized just like all the subhumans they have seen behind barbed wire, or hanging up lifeless from meathooks in meat markets.

The airship captain manages to escape and finds his way toward a body of water, an ocean perhaps. There he sees lying face down in the water the Statue of Liberty. It is quite recognizable, in spite of being in wrecked decay. Only then does he realize something most horrible of all: his spaceship did not land on a strange planet, but back on earth itself. Somehow the flight had gone wrong; they had crash landed back on earth again, but they had passed through some kind of time warp so that it was years in the future.

Perhaps because of nuclear or biological warfare only a few remaining human beings had become animal-like, and they had been replaced by apes. The thing which made all this horror so perfectly clear was the ruins of such a recognizable, famous, and beloved landmark as the Statue of Liberty.

If the moving picture *Planet of the Apes* had been filmed in France, the wrecked object might have been the Eiffel Tower; in England, the clock tower of Big Ben at Westminster Abbey; in India, the Taj Mahal; in Rome, Saint Peter's Cathedral; in any country, whatever building represents the pride of its citizens: their hopes, dreams, history, and their spiritual values.

In Jerusalem in the days of Jesus and his disciples that building would have been the Temple. The Temple was their Statue of Liberty, their Eiffel Tower, their Westminster Abbey, their Taj Mahal, their Saint Peter's Cathedral. Imagine then how the disciples felt when Jesus said about the Jerusalem Temple in today's Gospel Lesson, "As for these things that you see, the days will come when not one stone will be left upon another; all will be thrown down."

As a matter of fact, destruction of the Jerusalem Temple is exactly what happened some 35 or forty years later. Between the years 66 and 70 A.D., the Jews rebelled against the Romans. It took four years for Rome to reconquer Jerusalem; but the Jews lost again, and this time Rome really destroyed Jerusalem. The only thing left of the Temple was a section of wall which is believed to be the Wailing Wall of Jerusalem where Jews are accustomed to gather still today, especially on Fridays, and bewail the fall of Jerusalem and the destruction of the Temple at least three times: in 586 B.C., 70 A.D., and 135 A.D.

One interpretation of today's Gospel Lesson is that Jesus' prediction came true in 70 A.D., and that could be the end of the prediction.

All those bad things in today's Gospel Lesson indeed happened before 70 A.D.:

- "Many will come in my name and say ... 'The time is near.'"
- "Nation will rise against nation, and kingdom against kingdom."

- "There will be great earthquakes, and in various places famines and plagues."
- "There will be dreadful portents and great signs from heaven."
- "They will arrest you and persecute you."
- "You will be betrayed even by parents and brothers, by relatives and friends."
- "And they will put some of you to death."

Jesus also had words of encouragement for his followers who were about to endure such bad things.

- "This will give you an opportunity to testify."
- "... I will give you words and a wisdom that none of your opponents will be able to withstand or contradict."
- "But not a hair of your head will perish." (This promise is hard to understand in relation to some of the above-mentioned bad things.)
- "By your endurance you will gain your souls."

Most of us would feel very relieved if we could simply dismiss today's Gospel Lesson as something which is strictly in the *past* tense — over and done with. It would certainly be reassuring that Jesus knew what he was talking about, that his prediction came so terribly true within forty years. It would make Jesus' other predictions so credible, so to-be-taken-seriously.

Even if that is the case, however, there are still lessons for you and me to take to heart.

What about destruction of our world's environment here in a new century and a new millennium? We can look at before-and-after photographs in our nature magazines of forests, fields, rivers, lakes, and cities every bit as depressing as a fallen Statue of Liberty or "thrown down" Temple. We should be ashamed and frightened of what we have done to God's world before our children and grandchildren get their chance to live in it.

What about our loss of personal integrity, self-discipline, and self-sacrifice? Why is it that what we used to call "family values" are now mocked and ridiculed in public entertainment? In all these fearful things (both 70 A.D. and 2001 A.D.) we have Jesus' assurance, "By your endurance you will save your souls."

A state legislature was in session when a summer storm so darkened the sky that it seemed like night even in midday. "It's the end of the world!" shouted one frightened representative. "Bring out candles," ordered the Speaker of the House. "If this is indeed the Second Coming of Christ, I would like him to find us hard at our work."

Saint Francis was hoeing in the monastery garden one day, when a fellow monk asked him, "Francis, what would you do now, if you knew for a fact that the world would end this very afternoon?" "I would just keep on hoeing in this garden," he said.

Seminary students were engaged in a discussion of what Bible text they would choose for their final sermon, if they had reason to believe that this was the Final Day. Some suggested John 3:16, "For God so loved the world that he gave his only Son, so that everyone who believes in him may not perish but may have eternal life."

Others suggested Psalm 23, "The Lord is my shepherd, I shall not want ... Even though I walk through the darkest valley I fear no evil...."

Still others suggested the very last verses of the Bible, Revelation 22:20-21, "The one who testifies to these things says, 'Surely I am coming soon.' Amen. Come, Lord Jesus! The grace of the Lord Jesus be with all the saints. Amen."

The winning suggestion was, "I would preach on whatever Bible lesson was appointed for the Gospel for the day."

A homeowner had hired a gardener to plant a certain kind of tree. "But that kind of tree takes many years to mature," the gardener protested. "Then get started with the planting," the homeowner replied. "You do not have a moment to lose."

The common factor in all these stories is the importance of doing God's will all the time, so that there is no need for panic or hurry when any emergency comes — even the end of the world.

The final words of today's Gospel Lesson give us all the assurance we need to trust God: "By your endurance you will gain your souls."

All Saints' Sunday

Golden Rule Saints

Luke 6:20-31

On All Saints' Sunday there is a pastor who likes to take a camera into the pulpit with her. She tells the congregation that she wants some snapshots of modern, living saints. Not artists' conceptions of long-ago saints with old-fashioned clothes and halos around their heads — but today-saints. Then she snaps pictures (with flash) of the entire congregation, from left-to-right.

The congregation is startled the first time, because they have heard of Saint Matthew, Saint Mark, Saint Luke, and Saint John — but the people here in church today?

Nevertheless, most Protestants are supposed to believe that all Christians are saint and sinner at the same time. In spite of our sins, we church-going Christians are indeed "saints." In the words of Martin Luther, God "calls, gathers, enlightens, and sanctifies the whole Christian church on earth, and keeps it united with Jesus Christ in the one true faith."

Our Roman Catholic brothers and sisters — with all proper respect — seem to believe that saints need to be special people. More than 2,000 of these special people saints are listed in a layman's concise biographical dictionary of the saints. Keep in mind that this difference in interpreting saints is nothing to get all upset about. It is just one of the differences that make church life interesting.

There was a pharmacist in a small corner drug store; some affectionately called him "the funny druggist." He saluted occasional clergy-customers with a "Happy Saint Swithin Day!" greeting. "Was there really a Saint Swithin, and who was he?" a clergy-shopper wondered. Sure enough, he found Saint Swithin in a church history book. Saint Swithin was a bishop in Winchester, England, who lived more than 1,100 years ago. Saint Swithin performed small miracles — restoring, for example, a basketful of broken eggs which had been dropped by an old woman in the market.

"I found Saint Swithin," the pastor told the pharmacist. "July 15 is Saint Swithin Day." "You mean there really was a Saint Swithin?" the druggist asked. "I thought it was just something funny to say."

So we have Saint Matthew, Saint Mark, Saint Luke, Saint John, Saint Swithin, 2,000 more special people saints in a biographical dictionary — plus everybody here in church today.

For many of our church denominations today's proper altar color is white. It is a reminder of a description in Revelation 7:9 of that great reunion we look forward to heaven:

> *After this I looked, and behold, a great multitude which no man could number, from every nation, from all tribes and peoples and tongues, standing before the throne and before the Lamb, clothed in white robes....*

Today's Gospel has a list of saintly characteristics:

> *Blessed are you who are poor, for yours is the kingdom of God. Blessed are you who are hungry now, for you will be filled. Blessed are you who weep now, for you will laugh. Blessed are you when people hate you ... on account of the Son of Man.*

At first glance today's Gospel appears to be that beloved passage of Scripture known as The Beatitudes, but today's Gospel takes a less familiar nasty turn with its list of "woes":

> *But woe to you who are rich; for you have received your consolation. Woe to you who are full now, for you will be hungry. Woe to you who are laughing now, for you will mourn and weep. Woe to you when all speak well of you....*

What happened here? With just a little study we remember that The Beatitudes which we love and sometimes memorize come from Matthew 5:3-11. No doubt both Matthew and Luke have given us true quotations from Jesus. For some reason Matthew chose to emphasize the positive; Luke balanced it with some negatives.

An alumnus' description of his fiftieth high school class reunion sheds some light here. He had graduated from high school in 1951, and his graduating class had its share of beautiful people: the class kings and queens, the football and basketball stars, the cheerleaders, and the "socials." There had also been the scholars, the loners, the less than attractive ones, and mostly the unknown and unremembered.

What would they all look like now, fifty years later? He discovered in a surprising number of instances that now they looked and acted just about the same as each other. Many of the kings and queens had aged ungracefully, and many of the loners had blossomed into attractive happiness. Aging and time had been great levelers.

On All Saints' Sunday we consider among other things what we are now, and what we will be in the next world. Today's Gospel tells us that death and resurrection are the great levelers. Status things which seem so important to us now — money, gourmet food, entertainment, and popularity — should not seem important to us saints in this world; and they will be worthless when we are saints in the next world. That is the reason Jesus said both the "blesseds" and the "woes" in today's Gospel.

We live in a time when winning and success are so important, that coaches who lose too many games are fired, the bottom line of a company's profit-or-loss statement gets the most attention from stockholders, and even congregations are judged as "successful" or "unsuccessful" by comparing this year's average attendance with last year's. All Saints' Sunday is a good time for us to hear once again the words of an old-time sports writer who wrote these words which sadly seem embarrassingly quaint today: "And when that Great Scorer comes to write against your name, He will ask not if you won or lost, but how you played the game."

Outside Jordanville, New York, is a Russian Orthodox monastery and seminary. It is hard to find, and its Byzantine-Russian architecture, golden onion-shaped domes, and black-robed monks make visitors feel out of place and out of the twenty-first century. Everything is Old World Russian, including the cemetery with its row on row of grave markers: Orthodox crosses with a short horizontal piece above our more familiar armspiece, and with an off-angled footpiece closer to the bottom. Except for the names of the people buried there, every gravemarker cross is the same. That cemetery is a witness to All Saints' Sunday's description of the next world, where there is no rank and no privilege.

Today's Gospel also contains The Golden Rule: "Do to others as you would have them do to you." People who shop at Penney stores may remember that their founder, J. C. Penney, while he was alive, tried to operate his stores "according to the Golden Rule." J. C. Penney tried to treat his employees properly, sold good quality merchandise at fair prices, and used his own wealth in generous ways.

Historians of Toledo, Ohio, speak of "Golden Rule" Jones, who was an enlightened manufacturer ahead of his time. He provided picnic tables for his employees and their lunch boxes at mealtimes. There was also a park for employees' families on holidays. Sam "Golden Rule" Jones became mayor of Toledo, Ohio, from 1897-1904.

Some of our church books of worship have included names of men and women for "commemorations": Martin Luther King, Jr., Martin Luther, John Wesley, Charles Wesley, Dietrich Bonhoeffer, John Calvin, Pope John XXIII, Johann Sebastian Bach, Florence Nightingale, Albert Schweitzer, Henry Melchior Muhlenberg, and George Frederick Handel. We do not put the word *Saint* in front of their names, but they are part of the communion of saints we celebrate today.

At our church conventions once a year we hear read the names of pastors who have died during the preceding twelve months. Usually we sing the hymn "For All The Saints." Every pastor there knows that some day his or her name will be read aloud, and others will do the singing:

Oh may your soldiers, faithful, true, and bold,
Fight as the saints who nobly fought of old
And win with them the victor's crown of gold.
Alleluia! Alleluia!

We are thankful today for all the saints who have gone before us and prepared things for us. We want to be saints like them.

Christ The King Sunday

The Throne Of The Cross

Luke 23:33-43

Kings are not what they used to be. In Bible days there were kings of Israel and caesars of Rome. In more recent history there were czars of Russia, kings of France, emperors of the Holy Roman Empire, and kaisers of Germany. They all were powerful and privileged, but they are gone now.

Even the royal family of England has had to reinvent itself to win the support of English taxpayers. Verse three of "Onward Christian Soldiers" has proven truer than its nineteenth-century author could ever have imagined:

> *Crowns and thrones may perish,*
> *Kingdoms rise and wane,*
> *But the Church of Jesus*
> *Constant will remain.*

Some of the power and majesty we once attributed to kings is now imitated by stars of television, music, sports, and Hollywood. Today's shakers and movers are politicians, bankers, and chief executive officers of giant corporations.

It is no accident that a rock musical of some years ago took for its title, *Jesus Christ, Superstar.* If you and I were really trying to be modern and so-called "relevant," we might very well change the name of this last Sunday of the church year from "Christ the King" to "Christ the Superstar," or perhaps, "Jesus, C.E.O. of the Universe."

Let us, however, preserve enough dignity and tradition to keep "Christ the King" as our name for this last Sunday of the church year.

There is a pastor who prepares little paper crowns for today's children's sermon. In addition to the colors of precious stones, the words "King Jesus" appear on the little crowns. Children are invited to take two crowns per child — one to take home, and one to hang on the head or arms of a suitable altar cross.

It seems strange to have a Good Friday lesson this close to Christmas-time. Two of Good Friday's Seven Last Words are quoted in today's Gospel Lesson: "Father, forgive them, for they do not know what they are doing," and "Truly I tell you, today you will be with me in Paradise."

We sometimes accuse advertisers of "rushing the seasons." Christ the King Sunday seems to *leapfrog* the next seasons of Advent, Christmas, Epiphany, and Lent — running right into next Holy Week itself.

Actually Christ the King Sunday does not leapfrog the next three-and-a-half months at all; it summarizes the past twelve months. Wrapped up in today's Gospel is the infant king of *last* Christmas: "Hark! The herald angels sing, 'Glory to the newborn *king.*'"

The mocking of the soldiers in today's Gospel ("If you are the King of the Jews, save yourself!") is an echo of last winter's First Sunday in Lent, when the devil dared to goad Jesus, "If you are the Son of God, command this stone to become a loaf of bread" (Luke 4:3). And again, "If you are the Son of God, throw yourself down from here ... " (Luke 4:9).

Indeed, all of Jesus' parables, miracles, and sermons of the past twelve months are focused today on the throne of the cross.

There was a high school textbook which ended each chapter with a summary. Lazy students tried to take shortcuts by reading the summary without reading its preceding chapter. It did not work well as a substitute, but for the students who had read the chapter diligently, the summary was a good condensation of the preceding seven or eight pages. Similarly, today's Gospel is a summary of the twelve months we have just finished.

Christ the King Sunday reminds us of our need for reconciliation with God.

A few years ago we heard high level apologies for historic sins. Lutherans apologized to Jewish people for Martin Luther's anti-Semitic writings in the 1540s. Roman Catholics and Lutherans apologized to each other for the unpleasant things our ancestors said to each other some 460 years ago.

The United States apologized to our citizens of Japanese descent who were forced into internment camps in some of our western states during World War II. (Their loyalty had been doubted in our war against Japan.) Baptists apologized to African-Americans, because Baptists had supported slavery before the Civil War.

All these apologies revealed an uneasiness about past sins; but the apologies seemed too little and too late. "You cannot *un*ring a bell," says an old proverb. We end up confessing somebody else's sins; and these apologies leave us wondering (at least they *should* leave us wondering) what bad things you and I are doing today that will make future generations apologize for us. Next, we should stop doing these bad things right now!

Perhaps future generations will feel the need to apologize for our running up the national debt for our grandchildren to pay off. Perhaps they will apologize for our cutting down too many trees, and then covering the earth with blacktop.

Will our as yet unborn apologists say, "Sorry!" for our heating up the globe, or for driving too many cars? Will it be because we are tolerating a system of government which leaves such feelings of hopelessness that so few people even care to vote? "There's not a nickel's worth of difference between the two parties," complained one independent presidential candidate. And "People get the politicians they deserve," wrote a newspaper columnist.

In all these things, and no doubt many more, we need to repeat the words of the tax collector in Jesus' parable, "God, be merciful to me, a sinner!" (Luke 18:13).

Thank God for his forgiveness through Jesus' death on the cross. Christ the King Sunday reminds us of our need for reconciliation with God.

Christ the King Sunday also reminds us of our need for reconciliation with each other.

All *good* kings wanted their subjects to like each other. Bad kings did not care, just so long as people obeyed royal edicts and paid royal taxes. As a good king, Christ wants us to like each other. All people who are loyal to Christ the King should find ways to get along with each other. A theologian said, "When we gather to kneel at the foot of Jesus' cross, we also get closer to each other."

Although we Christians disagree about answers to the question "What would Jesus do?" we should be able to disagree and to discuss with respect and love. We may need at times to be "the loyal opposition," as a minority in Christ the King's house of parliament.

We should keep in mind that if we act considerately and intelligently, it should be unnecessary to have lots of reconciliation all the time. There is some truth at least to the advice of a saintly church-going mother, "If folks don't like you or me, the fault with us is likely to be."

An advice columnist listed a number of "inviting" personal behaviors for us to learn to imitate: a relaxed posture, smiling, listening carefully, shaking hands, opening a door for someone, being on time, sending a thoughtful note, accepting praise graciously, learning names, and waiting your turn.

Next the columnist listed "disinviting" personal behaviors for us to unlearn: interrupting, looking at your watch, scowling and frowning, slamming a door, using ridicule, making fun of a person, laughing at someone's misfortune, mimicking, being late, shoving ahead.

These "inviting" and "disinviting" personal behaviors are not mere tips from a how-to book on winning friends and influencing people; they can help us learn how to be good subjects of Christ the King. Christ the King Sunday reminds us of our need for reconciliation with each other.

> *O Jesus, king most wonderful!*
> *O Conqueror renowned!*
> *O Source of peace ineffable,*
> *In whom all joys are found.*
> — Bernard of Clairvaux

Thanksgiving Day

For What God Has Given

John 6:25-35

Thanksgiving, according to one newspaper columnist, has kept its original meaning better than any other holiday. That original meaning, he wrote, was family reunions around large dinner tables.

In contrast, Christmas has changed into Santa Claus and Rudolph the Red-Nosed Reindeer. Easter has come to emphasize new spring clothes and the Easter bunny. Even our national holidays — Memorial Day, Fourth of July, and Labor Day — have become cook-outs and summer travel get-aways.

But what about Thanksgiving? Those of us here in a Thanksgiving church service may be surprised that family reunions around large dinner tables would be considered Thanksgiving's original meaning; but after a little thought that description seems not too bad.

For one thing, it fits the picture of our Pilgrim ancestors getting together with Native American-Indians. The Indians, we think, brought deer meat and wild turkey to the first Thanksgiving, while the Pilgrims brought sweet potatoes, bread, cranberry sauce, and pumpkin pie. Most important, that first harvest celebration seemed to be a time of peace and harmony among the European immigrants and the Native Americans. So-called Indian Wars had not started yet.

For another thing, today's Thanksgiving reunions bring out thankful feelings about our blessings. We may even sing a few Thanksgiving hymns: "We gather together to ask the Lord's blessing" or "Come, ye thankful people, come; raise the song of harvest-home" or "Now thank we all our God with heart and hands and voices."

For still another thing, today's Thanksgiving gives us some probably-deserved feelings of guilt: "We have so much. What should we do for people who have so little?" we ask ourselves. So we try to ease these guilty feelings by donating Thanksgiving baskets to less fortunate people. Fund raisers for soup kitchens and feeding programs know that Thanksgiving is a good time to ask us for money, because we will enjoy our Thanksgiving dinners better, if we have given them some cash or a check.

Now there is a new kind of Thanksgiving guilt which comes from our historical mistreatment of American Indians. A thought-provoking question is, "Would our Pilgrim ancestors have been as kind to the Indians at that first Thanksgiving, as the Indians were to the Pilgrims, if their positions had been reversed?" In other words, "If the Pilgrims had been here first, and if Indian immigrants had arrived on the Mayflower, would the Pilgrims have allowed them a Thanksgiving feast at all, even providing the meat?" The unhappy suspicion is that they would have said, "No," to the savages.

That is enough Thanksgiving history and guilt-talk. It is time for our Bible lesson from the sixth chapter of John. In the preceding Bible verses Jesus had just finished feeding 5,000 people with only five loaves of bread and two fish. There were even twelve baskets of food left over, which Jesus directed his disciples to gather up so that there would be no waste.

Then the miracle, which Jesus intended to be a good gift, took an ugly turn. The idea of free food from Jesus was so appealing that the people wanted to make Jesus their king — in exchange, of course, for free food always. Jesus tried to get away from them by crossing the Sea of Galilee, but the crowd followed. When they caught up, they got to the point of their pursuit: "Sir, give us this bread always."

Jesus tried unsuccessfully to direct their crude request into something spiritual: "I am the bread of life. Whoever comes to me will never be hungry, and whoever believes in me will never be thirsty." The people felt those words were unsatisfactory, and a few verses after today's Gospel Lesson the crowd turned against

Jesus: "Then the Jews began to complain about him because he said, 'I am the bread that came down from heaven.' "

Let us, you and me, in this Thanksgiving season try once again to be grateful to God for all that we have received. We should remember that there is a big difference between what we need, and what we want. Our needs include just enough food, clothing, and shelter to keep us alive and healthy. Anything more is extra blessing.

A nutritionist distributed small dessert plates exactly six inches in diameter, the kind we would use for a piece of pie or cake. "There is enough space on that plate for a day's supply of food," the nutritionist said. Hard to believe! Even if the nutritionist is guilty of exaggeration, the general idea is correct — that we eat more than we need, and we expect our food to be tasty and good-looking besides.

A history of World War II described food rationing in war-time England. Because of the war, and because of enemy submarines sinking ships, food was short; everybody was a little hungry all the time. Keep in mind that the English people were not being starved in concentration camps, or in death camps, or in prisoner of war camps. They were just a little hungry all the time.

So how was the health of the average English person on August 15, 1945, when World War II ended? Answer: health was at its best, and better than it would become during peacetime prosperity. Most English people — and most United States people — eat more than we need. Our wants exceed our needs.

A missionary to a poor country told of a community-wide potluck supper, where the missionaries were invited to serve themselves first. The food looked so good, that they heaped their plates in good old-fashioned USA church potluck style. Only as they started to eat did they notice that the food supply at the supper table was barely adequate for everybody else. Nobody complained; nobody had an empty plate; nobody even looked at them with hostility, because they were honored guests. In the next suppers, however, the missionaries took only the amount of food they really needed. That was what everybody else did, just as a matter of normal living. For most of us our wants exceed our needs.

This Thanksgiving sermon is not intended to be a lecture on the dangers of being overweight, or the virtues of dieting, but to illustrate how our thankfulness has unfortunately demanded much more than we really need. A successful but unlikeable man boasted, "I want two of everything." His wants included two houses, two boats, two cars, two women, two of everything.

On Thanksgiving we — you and I — should be thankful for what God has given us, and then we should make good use of whatever that is.

> *I prayed for a bunch of fresh flowers, but I got an ugly cactus with many thorns.*
>
> *I prayed for beautiful butterflies, but got ugly worms.*
>
> *But the cactus grew lovely blooms, and the worms were caterpillars which became lovely butterflies.*
>
> *That is God's way.*

We also need to remember that we live through change; some are changes for the better, and some are for the worse. We would like to keep the best things of the past, plus gaining the advantages of the present. Sorry, it does not work that way. A lady visiting in a hospital looked at the park across the street from the main entrance. She recalled her childhood, when she played on that playground, while her father visited her sick mother.

It seems strange now, but children were not allowed inside hospitals in those days, unless they were sick themselves and admitted as patients. They were not even allowed to visit a sick mother, which is a bad memory of the so-called "good old days."

On the other hand, it was safe in those days to leave a child in a public playground. Unthinkable now! Too many speeding cars, and too many child molesters.

Here is how this story connects with our Thanksgiving. We would like to have the advantages of the past, plus gaining the advantages of the present, but it seems we do not get both.

A woman moved from a hilly part of Massachusetts to a flat part of Ohio. She missed the beauty of the Massachusetts hills, but she learned to enjoy instead the beautiful sunrises and sunsets of Ohio's open skies. When God provides for us there are often changes. We gain some things, and we lose others. There is gaining and losing.

This Thanksgiving let us be grateful for the miracles by which God provides for our needs — and so much more.

Lectionary Preaching After Pentecost

Virtually all pastors who make use of the sermons in this book will find their worship life and planning shaped by one of two lectionary series. Most mainline Protestant denominations, along with clergy of the Roman Catholic Church, have now approved — either for provisional or official use — the three-year Revised Common (Consensus) Lectionary. This family of denominations includes United Methodist, Presbyterian, United Church of Christ and Disciples of Christ. Recently the ELCA division of Lutheranism also began following the Revised Common Lectionary. This change has been reflected in the headings and Scripture listings with each sermon in this book.

Roman Catholics and Lutheran divisions other than ELCA follow their own three-year cycle of texts. While there are divergences between the Revised Common and Roman Catholic/Lutheran systems, the gospel texts show striking parallels, with few text selections evidencing significant differences. Nearly all the Gospel texts included in this book will, therefore, be applicable to worship and preaching planning for clergy following either lectionary.

A significant divergence does occur, however, in the method by which specific Gospel texts are assigned to specific calendar days. The Revised Common and Roman Catholic Lectionaries accomplish this by counting backwards from Christ the King (Last Sunday after Pentecost), discarding "extra" texts from the front of the list: Lutherans (not using the Revised Common Lectionary) follow the opposite pattern, counting forward from The Holy Trinity, discarding "extra" texts at the end of the list.

The following index will aid the user of this book in matching the correct text to the correct Sunday during the Pentecost portion of the church year.

(Fixed dates do not pertain to Lutheran Lectionary)

Fixed Date Lectionaries	**Lutheran Lectionary**
Revised Common (including ELCA) and Roman Catholic	*Lutheran*
The Day of Pentecost	The Day of Pentecost
The Holy Trinity	The Holy Trinity
May 29-June 4 — Proper 4, Ordinary Time 9	Pentecost 2
June 5-11 — Proper 5, Ordinary Time 10	Pentecost 3
June 12-18 — Proper 6, Ordinary Time 11	Pentecost 4
June 19-25 — Proper 7, Ordinary Time 12	Pentecost 5

June 26-July 2 — Proper 8, Ordinary Time 13	Pentecost 6
July 3-9 — Proper 9, Ordinary Time 14	Pentecost 7
July 10-16 — Proper 10, Ordinary Time 15	Pentecost 8
July 17-23 — Proper 11, Ordinary Time 16	Pentecost 9
July 24-30 — Proper 12, Ordinary Time 17	Pentecost 10
July 31-Aug. 6 — Proper 13, Ordinary Time 18	Pentecost 11
Aug. 7-13 — Proper 14, Ordinary Time 19	Pentecost 12
Aug. 14-20 — Proper 15, Ordinary Time 20	Pentecost 13
Aug. 21-27 — Proper 16, Ordinary Time 21	Pentecost 14
Aug. 28-Sept. 3 — Proper 17, Ordinary Time 22	Pentecost 15
Sept. 4-10 — Proper 18, Ordinary Time 23	Pentecost 16
Sept. 11-17 — Proper 19, Ordinary Time 24	Pentecost 17
Sept. 18-24 — Proper 20, Ordinary Time 25	Pentecost 18
Sept. 25-Oct. 1 — Proper 21, Ordinary Time 26	Pentecost 19
Oct. 2-8 — Proper 22, Ordinary Time 27	Pentecost 20
Oct. 9-15 — Proper 23, Ordinary Time 28	Pentecost 21
Oct. 16-22 — Proper 24, Ordinary Time 29	Pentecost 22
Oct. 23-29 — Proper 25, Ordinary Time 30	Pentecost 23
Oct. 30-Nov. 5 — Proper 26, Ordinary Time 31	Pentecost 24
Nov. 6-12 — Proper 27, Ordinary Time 32	Pentecost 25
Nov. 13-19 — Proper 28, Ordinary Time 33	Pentecost 26 Pentecost 27
Nov. 20-26 — Christ the King	Christ the King

Reformation Day (or last Sunday in October) is October 31 (Revised Common, Lutheran)

All Saints' Day (or first Sunday in November) is November 1 (Revised Common, Lutheran, Roman Catholic)

Books In This Cycle C Series

GOSPEL SET

Praying For A Whole New World
Sermons For Advent/Christmas/Epiphany
William G. Carter

Living Vertically
Sermons For Lent/Easter
John N. Brittain

Changing A Paradigm — Or Two
Sermons For Sundays After Pentecost (First Third)
Glenn E. Ludwig

Topsy-Turvy: Living In The Biblical World
Sermons For Sundays After Pentecost (Middle Third)
Thomas A. Renquist

Ten Hits, One Run, Nine Errors
Sermons For Sundays After Pentecost (Last Third)
John E. Berger

FIRST LESSON SET

The Presence In The Promise
Sermons For Advent/Christmas/Epiphany
Harry N. Huxhold

Deformed, Disfigured, And Despised
Sermons For Lent/Easter
Carlyle Fielding Stewart III

Two Kings And Three Prophets For Less Than A Quarter
Sermons For Sundays After Pentecost (First Third)
Robert Leslie Holmes

What If What They Say Is True?
Sermons For Sundays After Pentecost (Middle Third)
John W. Wurster

A Word That Sets Free
Sermons For Sundays After Pentecost (Last Third)
Mark Ellingsen

SECOND LESSON SET
You Have Mail From God!
Sermons For Advent/Christmas/Epiphany
Harold C. Warlick, Jr.

Hope For The Weary Heart
Sermons For Lent/Easter
Henry F. Woodruff

A Hope That Does Not Disappoint
Sermons For Sundays After Pentecost (First Third)
Billy D. Strayhorn

Big Lessons From Little-Known Letters
Sermons For Sundays After Pentecost (Middle Third)
Kirk W. Webster

Don't Forget This!
Robert R. Kopp
Sermons For Sundays After Pentecost (Last Third)

www.ingramcontent.com/pod-product-compliance
Lightning Source LLC
Chambersburg PA
CBHW061252040426
42444CB00010B/2359